WHEN GOD SPEAKS

Volume 1

Hara Saadia

ISBN 979-8-88685-118-2 (paperback)
ISBN 979-8-88685-119-9 (digital)

Christian Faith Publishing
832 Park Avenue
Meadville, PA 16335
www.christianfaithpublishing.com

Printed in the United States of America

PREFACE

Everything requires learning, and so does our relationship with God. When you are touched by God, the first thing you want to do is to get to know Him better. This learning is done not only through reading the word but also through prayer. Prayer is a key word in the Bible. It appears several times in the Bible chapters. In my childhood, I still remember my mother's voice which reminded me several times to pray in the morning when I woke up and at night when I went to bed. As a child, I did it without knowing the real purpose. But as I grew up in my spiritual life, I learned the importance of prayer and to appreciate more and more the presence of God in my life.

Prayer can be defined as the means of communicating with God. Our Heavenly Father is wonderful because he knew that we will need to talk with Him, and He simply asks us to pray. I like to compare prayer to a telephone device. Nowadays, the telephone has become an essential thing to communicate more quickly with our families and friends who are near us or millions of kilometers away. Well, prayer plays the same role; but instead of communicating with our loved ones, it puts us in direct contact with God.

To maintain relationships, we always need to communicate and to listen to the people around us. Well, God wants the same thing with us. He wants to talk to us, listen to us, and respond to our requests and supplications. Let us not forget that it is also our weapon of fight because when we pray, the distance between heaven and earth disappears and we can thus see the glory of God not only in our lives but also on earth while destroying the works of Satan.

Prayer allows us to have greater intimacy with God and to remain in His plans.

I always like to refer to 1 Thessalonians 5:17 where the apostle Paul asks the Thessalonians to "pray without ceasing." These verses show us that prayer is an obligation and not a choice and that it is of great importance.

Our whole life must be made of prayer whether in our studies, in our families, in our activities, or at work. We must never stop praying; it is a full-time job with great heavenly remuneration. It also allows us to stay connected to our God all the time since our life and relationship with God must be full-time and not part-time.

The texts that are part of this book were received during my moments of prayer and worship. They show that God speaks, and He still wants to talk to us more if we take the time to listen to Him and spend time in His presence. He is a living God, and He wants us to get closer to Him.

During your reading, my wish is that the Lord may speak to you personally and that He may reveal Himself to you.

When I close my eyes
I can only see your kindness and light
You are the alpha and omega
You are the Christ
You are the King of kings
The Holy of holies, the Lord of lords
Open my eyes to your glory, oh, God
Let me see your power
Creator of the universe
I can only bow down to your glory
To be amazed by your power
Savior of humanity
Come to my rescue, Jesus
Surround me with your presence and love
Enlighten me and purify me with your spirit
May all glory and worship be yours, my God

Sinner that I am
You saved me by dying on the cross
You offered me eternal life by reaching out to me
Why hesitate?
To take your hand, to enter the light
Drink this water of life and cover me with this cloak of glory
I don't know, Jesus
The world is holding me back
The darkness attracts me
Come to my rescue, Jesus
Deliver me from the oppressor
Lead me to the light paths
Where your grace reigns and your power shines
My soul calls you, but my body resists
I want to serve you, Jesus, but I don't know how to do it
Come to my rescue, Father
Be attentive to my distress
Because I'm nothing without you
Your child calls you, oh, Father
Give me your hand
And lead me to your light.

Over there in the sky
There is a mighty, eternal God
Who wants to know you
He wants to love you, teach you, enlighten you
Tell you the way to follow him
He is the King of kings, the Lord of lords
Alpha and omega
Now scream to him
He'll answer you, tell you what to do
I want to cry out to heaven, Lord, fill me
Transform my life, I need you
I want to scream to the sky
To acclaim you, to honor you, to proclaim your name
Wherever I would go
Acknowledge that you are God
The way of life
In you, there's everything
No one can compare to you

Every morning
I look in the mirror
In order to probe the depth of my soul
Who am I? Who am I?
That is the question I ask myself
I seek my identity, oh, God
The call you have for my life
I was not born for so little
I'm tired of the crumbs
I want to drink more of this water of life
Shine for your kingdom
Experience unforgettable things in your presence
Renew me, oh, God
My soul sighs for you
My heart seeks your ways
Fill me with a new anointing
In order to achieve great things for your kingdom
And live my Christian life to the fullest.

Regenerate me, Holy Spirit
Renew my thoughts
Revive me, restore my body
Because I'm weak
Revitalize me, Spirit of God
Fill me with your breath, oh, God
I want to feel the power of your spirit
This spirit of life and light
It's your spirit, oh, God
Who acts with power and glory
What a joy to see your Spirit in action
Spirit of truth, spirit of peace
I open my heart to you
Come to live in me, Holy Spirit.

When the wind blows
From east to west, from north to south
I am the there
Lends an ear to my whispers
They are as sweet as myrrh
Sunny and sparkling
I am in this breath
The breath of life
The breath of hope
A breath of joy and peace
Renewal will come through this breath
I will transform you and prepare you for my return
Shout out my name
Because I'm at the door
Prepare the feast for me
The meal of eternity.

Where did I get the help?
Help comes to me from the eternal
It is he who carries me and transports me
To a safe and protected place
He is my guardian
My shield and my armor
He's holding my hand
And makes me cross the valley of death
By leading me to green pastures
Where darkness has no place
Because his light shines eternally
Blessed be the name of my savior

You alone are my shield
My support, my armor
You are my source of life
The rock on which I rely
Open my heart, God
Make me sensitive to your voice
May my heart praise you
And my body loves you
Fill me with your mind
Rise me up with your power
May my eyes be opened to the immensity of your greatness
Oh, God, you are infinitely great
Majestic is your name
I want to know more about you
Stay close to you
Drink your word and your sweet whispers.

What a grace to worship you, my Lord
With heart and the depth of my soul
What joy to sing your praises, El Shaddai, until exhaustion
I want to glorify you until my last breath
This peace that invades me
When I adore you through the fibers of my body
Is comparable to nothing on this earth
I feel like I'm flying
I feel so satisfied
Oh, God, open my heart to worship you even more
I don't want to just recite the words
But to sing with life and all the respect you deserve
Because you are God, the Lord of lords
The light of this world
Come, Lord, I want to worship you until dawn
Dancing on your praise, shouting your magnificence
As did your servant David
Teach me to adore you, my Lord
Show me how to praise you, oh, God
While acknowledging your greatness.

You're so big, my God
That there are no words to describe you
Every day, you surprise me
By revealing yourself to me
By showing me your power
Your magnificence in a new way
And now I realize that
That I don't really know you
Teach me to humiliate myself, my Lord
To see beyond my person
Beyond the world and the fleshly laws
I want to discover the vastness of your greatness
Taste your power
To drink this water of life that is your spirit
Seeing the supernatural operated on in my life
My thoughts are limited, oh, God
Open my heart to receive heavenly thoughts
In order to see your miracle in my life.

Light of the world
I want to be blinded by you, my Lord
Take the veil off my eyes
Lighten my eyes
So that I may see your kingdom
Light a new flame in me
Who will devour me entirely
And will bring me out of the darkness
Shine in my life, oh, God
I need you to show me the way
Which leads to the source of life
I want to discover eternity
Sitting at your feet
To get drunk on your presence
To hear your voice and your sweet whispers
Attach myself to your word
To purify me with your Spirit
Get out of this hellhole and proclaim your name
Enlighten me, Adonai
Because you are God
I want to find the path that leads to eternity
In your presence.

The earth cries, Adonai
She shouts out her pain and sorrow
Where are you, my Lord?
Your people are in distress
A deep sadness
He doesn't know what to do
He's asking for help
But their eyes are not fixed on you
Your people need you, oh, God
Reveal yourself to them
Visit your people, Jesus
Wake us up with the power of your Holy Spirit
Teach us to meditate on your word
To realize that you're coming back soon
The world is falling apart, El Shaddai
But there is still hope
It is in you, Jesus
Open our eyes and hearts
To receive this eternal Truth.

Blessed is the one who praises me
Blessed be the one who adores me
My peace is upon him
I would bless him
And his house will be a house of joy
The angels camp around his house
He is surrounded by my presence and my light
Any word spoken against him shall have no effect
’Cause I’d break all the enemy’s arrows
I am his armor and shield
His protector and Lord
I will bless him for the rest of these days.

I've given you everything
What are you looking for in the world?
Let go so I can
Act freely
Don't resist my spirit
I want to change you and transform you
You lack faith and trust
Believe in me
Because I want to act in your lives
Open your spiritual eyes
To see my glory and power
Be thankful
Bless my name at all times.

I'm on a mountain
I'm looking for my way
But I can hardly find it
I'm trying to trust my instincts
But nothing to do, I can't find my way back
Where am I going?
I don't know, I don't know
I'm trying to do what everyone else does
Walk in the same direction as them
Why I feel lost, Lord
I feel in my heart this voice trying to show me the way
But I resist
Because I want to do like the others
My flesh is satisfied, but my soul torments me
Come and take my hand, oh, God
Show me the right direction
The one who will lead me to your kingdom
Where my soul will be at peace.

I desire more from you, my Lord
But I don't know how to do it
I want to know more about you
But I can't do it
Teach me, my Lord
Show me what to do
Open my heart to love you more
Everything distracts me from you, Adonai
Break the bonds, oh, God
Free me from the world
Attract me to you
Point my eyes at you
Come and take your rightful place
Take away everything that prevents my consecration
Teach me to obey you
To surrender myself totally to you
Take control of my life, oh, God
Lead me to the Promised Land.

Praise the Lord
Glorify him in spirit
Praise his name wherever you are
Acclaim him, proclaim his name
Witness his goodness, mercy, grace, and blessings in your lives
Bless him at all times
Pay tribute to him wherever you go
Honor him with your lives
Give up everything for him
Confide in him
Be committed to his word
Ask for his presence
He will enlighten you
And will lead you to his kingdom
Where you will discover its power
His greatness and holiness.

God's love is like sand seeds in the desert
Untouchable, incalculable, and always present
Every day we feel it
If we let him do it
He surrounds us with his presence
He wants us to be immersed in this love
Whatever our situations
This love is free of charge
Available for all
Let us declare God's love in our lives
He is a God of love and not of rejection
He accepts us as we are
And hugs us day after day
Let us be convinced of this love
Because he loves us more than a father
He cries when we are lost
He always wants to bring us back to him
So that we can live with him
Feel his affection for us
Facing the world with confidence
To proclaim this love on earth
Talking about him around us
Sharing this love with others.

How wonderful it is to know you, my Lord
Your greatness and immensity surprise me every day
Nothing is impossible for you, my God
I want to believe it and live it
Take away everything that limits me
And keeps me from seeing you act
Supernaturally and with power in my life
I want to see the God of Moses act in my life
See your miracles and wonders
Living supernatural healings
Open up more to you
Teach me to think like you, oh, God
Open my eyes to see
Spiritually and not fleshly
Use the spirit that is in me
This precious and inestimable gift
That you made me
Teach me to recognize the value of this present
Who lives in me and acts with power
I want to see with your eyes, oh, God
Connect me to you
Fill me with your presence
Renew me, enlighten me, El Shaddai
Teach me to appreciate, your majesty
Open my heart to receive the heavenly words.

The eternal is my shepherd
He sees my tears
And wipes them happily
He hugs me in his arms
And surrounds me with his love
I don't worry about anything
Because he has everything in control
He takes care of everything
He heals my wounds
And gives me peace of heart
He's standing me up
And pushes me to testify to his greatness
The price to pay is great
But he supports me and guides me along the thorny paths
I want to put my trust in him
Walk in his direction
Glorify his name for every tear shed
Because he sees my devotion.

What a magnificent God we serve
Always present for us
It supports us, restores us, and enlightens us
It is the alpha and omega
A God who does not forget us
A God who raises when we fall
A God who fills us with joy and peace at all times
A faithful God who always fulfills his promises
A God who never abandons us
A God who accepts us as we are
A God who wants us to discover eternity
A God of love and compassion
A helpful and protective God
A God who speaks to us
Oh, what a joy to know you, my Lord
Because you are a living God.

How difficult it is to serve you, my Lord
In recent times
I feel attacked and oppressed
When I want to surrender myself to you
My brothers reject me
I'm called crazy
When I talk about your power, your greatness
People look at me wrong, I'm rejected by your people
But I stand up and keep walking in your ways
'Cause you were rejected by your people, Jesus
Misunderstood by your family
Isolated and abandoned
While you were the son of the very high
The King of kings
The Lord of lords
I want to do like you, Jesus
Stay at the foot of the cross
Continue to proclaim your word
Whatever the obstacles.

Look around you
The earth and the sky
How can you doubt my existence?
I am God
I've done everything for you
So that you don't miss out on anything
I created you so that you would love me
Selfish as you are
You forgot me
You don't even know who I am
You continue to walk according to the world
The devil has blinded you
You don't recognize me anymore
But one day will come
That we'll know all over the world
That I am the eternal
On that day, all my creations will be restored
Those who have kept my commandments
Will live in abundance
Seek my ways
There is not much time left
Because I'll be back soon.

Let me transport you to my kingdom
I want to show you unknown lands
To make you discover unknown things
Call me, ask me
I will open my kingdom to you
I would transform you and prepare you
So that you're ready
For me and my kingdom
Believe with all your heart
Call me day and night
Open your heart to receive my word
Walk in my ways, I will reveal myself to you
Because I love you, and I want to know you
You are my child, and I am your creator, your father
I will guide you and show you hidden things
So then you didn't know about the existence
For I am God.

Hallelujah, Jesus
Glory be to you
May my soul adore you, Lord
Thank you for your presence
Blessed be your name, Yeshua
Savior of humanity
The Holy of holies
Alpha and omega
There are no words to describe you, Jesus
I want to kneel in front of your splendor
To recognize with all my heart
Your sacrifice on the cross
Your blood that was shed for me
And who broke my chains
Now I'm free to go
Like a bird
I want to take my flight with you, Jesus
To discover unknown lands
Be my eternal compass
Lead me to your kingdom.

I shout to you, my Lord
'Cause you're my God
I cry at your feet
Because you're the only one
Who understands my pain, my suffering
I tried it on my own
But I can't get out of it
I asked the men for help
Nothing to do
I can't find a solution
I turn to you, Father
You created me, and you know me
You know what I need
I should have come to you first
Forgive my unbelief
My pride and my carnal wisdom
I want to know your will
Give me your joy, Father
I don't want to hide anymore, Lord
I want to live in your truth
Learn to listen better to you
Giving you control of my life
Confide in you
When everything is good and when everything is bad
Because you are my creator, Lord
And you wait for your child to come to you
Thank you, God, for your love and trust.

Beautiful is my name
Glorious is my name
Raised me with all your heart
'Cause I am God
No one can compare to me
Bless my name with all your heart
Believe in my glory, my power, and I will act
Turn your eyes on me, and I'll answer you
I am God
Believe in me and in the impossible
'Cause I'm the God of the impossible
May my people bless my name
Yell at me, and I'll answer.

You are everything, I am nothing
I'm lost, you guide me
I'm sick, you heal me
I'm worried, you reassure me
When the doors close, you open them
I scream at you, you answer me
If I cry, you wipe my tears
You keep me company if I get lonely
I'm starving, you're feeding me
Thirsty, you give me the water of life
If I fall, you pick me up
You restore me when I'm shot and wounded
In my poverty, you enrich me and provide for all my needs
Oh, my Lord, you are a living God
Slow to anger and rich in goodness
Faithful and merciful
I look into heaven and earth
I realize that no one is comparable to you
Blessed be your name, Adonai.

I'm tired, my Lord
To run after the world
To try to please men
To do like the others
The disappointment is great
I don't recognize myself
Where is my identity, Lord?
Talk to me
I'm ready to listen to you
To obey you and act
Change me
Come and take your rightful place
Let me discover your wonders, Lord
I want to taste your grace, Adonai
And let me be transformed by your love.

I am the alpha and omega
Yell at me, and I'll answer you
Avoid false pretenses
'Cause I'm a God of truth
Be transparent in everything you do
I like the truth
Destroy the lie that is among you
Be pure and true
With me and your neighbors
Worship me in spirit and in truth
Avoid worshipping me in the flesh and lying
Because I'm not where there's the fake one
I am a God of truth and not of lies
Avoid taking action
To be seen by men
But do everything for my glory
Be sincere in everything
I am a God who loves
A sincere adoration that comes from the heart.

Come to me, Holy Spirit
Flood me with your presence
Fill me with your love
Lead me to the heavenly paths
Where my father lives
Where I can see your glory
And your power operated
Sweet Holy Spirit
I want to hear you talk to me
I want to feel your presence in me
I want to learn to listen to you
To trust you
To let myself be guided by you
To let you take control
Oh, Spirit of God
Thank you for your presence in me
I love you, Holy Spirit.

I am no longer a slave to sin
You broke my chains
You have delivered me from my enemies
You pulled me out of the darkness
To show me the light
I am your child, Lord
What a joy to belong to you
To see the light surrounding me entirely
To see the world of darkness shaking
And run away from me
I am in you, Jesus
You gave me your ability
Your authority and ability
Oh, Lord, what joy and peace to be your child
I float, and I can lift mountains
Because you live in me
It is not by my strength but by your power
Hallelujah, Jesus, and thank you for your Holy Spirit.

Why am I so proud?
I have no idea, Lord
I realize it's a second skin
This pride swells from day to day
I denigrate others, I think I am superior to them
Oh, Lord, come and humiliate me and deliver me from this sin
The first sin of the world
I am far from perfect, I am a sinner
But I can't recognize him in my condition
Teach me humility, oh, God
Simplicity, respect for yourself
Lower me down to take your rightful place in my life
Adonai, I want to be like a baby
Acknowledges that I am nothing
Destroys all the thoughts of the world inside me
I am far from perfect and sinless
I'm not a saint at all
I have spots on my body
Representing all my sins
Holiness and perfection come from you, Jesus
As long as I'm on this earth
You will continue to purify me and sanctify me
By your spirit and your word
Blessed be your name, Adonai
To show me my limits, my weaknesses
And make me see that in front of you
I am nothing
Thank you for your humility, Jesus.

I am who I am
The God of glory
The God of power
The God of holiness
Shout at me
I will listen to you and answer you
May my word be your truth
An armor, a shield against this world
May this word be engraved in your hearts
And let it come to life
It's perfect because it comes from me
Meditate day and night
So that it can remain in your memories
And come to life in your daily life
May this word be your slogan
In order to prepare you for my return.

Believe in me with all your heart
Because I'll answer you
I am a living God and not a dead God
Come to me with everything you have
I would reveal myself to you
I want to know you so much
Enter your privacy
Walking with you
I cry when you ignore me
Because I created you, and you are my child
I love you with all my being
This love I have for you
Is immense and inexhaustible
Come to me, my child
Come and discover my kingdom
I will fill you with joy and peace
I would bless you with my presence
I am your God, your father, your creator
And your savior.

My flesh is weak, Jesus
She is the source of all temptation
My soul aspires to more than you
But my body resists
Oh, Jesus, I'm weak
Teach me to walk with your mind
In order to eliminate any temptation
I can't do anything on my own
I am unable to resist
At the wishes of my chair
Purify me with your spirit, oh, God
Sanctify my body with your blood, Jesus
In order for it to be a suitable temple
For your Holy Spirit
Cause you're a saint, Jesus.

How can I thank you, Jesus
Of everything you've done for me
Your graces and blessings in my life
Are inexhaustible and incalculable
Oh, my Lord, thank you for everything
Give me a grateful heart
To praise you, to glorify you, and to witness
Of your works in my life
What a joy to be led by your Spirit
You're never wrong
Excellent is your name, Adonai
I want to be with you, Emmanuel
Shout your name on the earth
Thank you, Jesus, for coming to meet me
Thank you, Jesus, for your visit and your sacrifice on the cross
Thank you for your blood that broke my chains
Thank you for the New Jerusalem coming soon
Hallelujah for your return, Jesus, for whom we are waiting
impatiently.

I listened to you
Your screams and cries
Keep looking for me
I would blow on you
A new breath of fresh air
Bless my name
Seek my kingdom with faith
I will answer you and transform you
I'm here with you
Until the end of time.

When I see the beauty of the landscape
The balance between the planets and in the galaxy
The change of seasons, night and day
I can only glorify you
Your creation is beautiful and complete
Oh, God, let me see your greatness
I want to appreciate the beauty of your creation
And preserve this magnificent gift
Lord, I want to learn to appreciate what comes from you
Because everything that comes from you is beautiful and majestic
Complete and indescribable
Nothing compares to everything you do
Glory be to you for this beautiful work.

My heart cries, oh, God
I am saddened
To see the world ignore you
Your people have stopped looking for your ways
He does as he pleases
He no longer listens to you, their hearts are drawn to the world
He listens to the enemy's voice
He walks in the darkness
And rejects the light
Comes to our rescue, Jesus
Your people are desperate and discouraged
Wake us up, oh, God
You're at the door, Lord
We don't have much time left, Jesus
Fill us with your breath
Touch the depth of our soul, Adonai
Renew our thoughts, El Shaddai
Prepare us for your return, Jesus
In order for us to be ready to welcome you.

Here comes the dawn again
I seek your face, my Lord
I'm looking for your ways
Renew your graces in my life again
I rely on you, oh, God
I put my day in your hands
Lead me, protect me
Use me for your kingdom
Surround me with your presence
And by the power of your Holy Spirit
I want to receive your thoughts, El Shaddai
Before starting this day
You have so much to tell me, Father
Open my heart to receive the heavenly words
Teach me to obey and listen to you every day
Blessed be your name, Adonai
You, the creator of humanity.

You are the one who heals, oh, Lord
No one can compare to you
You are the eternal doctor
The greatest of all
Oh, Jesus, comes to heal us
We ask for it with faith
We want to see your hand act
Your glory shines forth
Seeing blind people being healed
And sick people standing up for your work
We pray for spiritual and physical healing
Comes to our rescue, Adonai
You are the one who holds our lives in your hands
You know when we'll be cured
You take care of us
Your hand is strong, oh, God
Comes to our rescue, Jesus
And free us from the hand of the oppressor
Destroys the arrows of the evil one
Who wants to reach us
Physically and morally
Lord, you are the King of kings
In you, we are always victorious
We demand our healing
And let us proclaim your name, Lord
Because you're the one who's healing.

Give yourself up, I am God
I will deliver you and show you the light
I am greater than darkness
Call my name with all your being
I will enlighten you with my light
And the darkness will run away from you
You're not made for the darkness
You're my child, and I love you
I'm here near you
Let me do it myself
You will be free from this burden
That you carry with you
I am God
The greatest of all
No one can compare to me
Seek the light
I'll show you the way.

Believe me, I'm with you
I'll give you more
Give me your heart
Call me, and I'll show you
The world of the Holy Spirit
A world of power
I am God, and I want to do more with my people
Keep calling me in your lives
Believe in me, I am everything
I want to change this generation
Because I'll be back soon
You must stand up and work for my kingdom
You have to wake up and walk with me
I am your Lord
Your God, the God of forgiveness
The God of power
Believe in me, and you will never be disappointed.

When I see your creation
I'm always surprised.
Because all your creation is beautiful and perfect
There is nothing in this world that can compare to your creation
Oh, God, I want to worship you and give you back all the glory
There's no one like you
I want to thank you for our lives and for everything
Thank you for your love, salvation, and sacrifice on the cross
You gave me your Holy Spirit
Every day I can get up
And to think that I'm your beloved child
You loved me so much, Lord
Every day, I want to sing your name
And give you everything I have.

Give me everything you have
You don't need to carry your burden
I am God, and I can do anything
You are my child
I love you so much
I even sacrificed my son for you
Fix your eyes on me
Don't be distracted
I am with you
I'm the only person you need to believe
You can trust me
I am your creator
My eyes are fixed on you
Don't be afraid
Of what the world thinks, neither men
You have me, and it's the only thing you need
I will protect you
I am with you, and my spirit is in you
Follow him, believe him
He is the best guide for you
He will guide you on the path of eternity
Where my light shines night and day
Now you are a child of God
A child of eternity and light
You are my soldier, and my hand is on you.

What can I do, my Lord?
Nothing at all
Because you are the one who creates in me the will and the
power
I can't do anything on my own
I have no desire to act
I realize that I'm just an empty shell
Without your spirit, I'm lost
Your mind pushes me
To do something for your kingdom
And act according to your direction, not mine
I don't want to displease you, Jesus
Help me to see more clearly for your kingdom
My thoughts are not necessarily yours, my God
Come and take full control, Jesus
Create in me the desire to know you better
Touch my heart, transform it in your image, Jesus.

Fill me with your spirit
Connect me back to you
I want to recharge my energy at your side
Renew my thoughts, oh, God
Every day is new
I'm getting to know you
I am living new adventures
You are a God who surprises
You like change
I know you so little, my Lord
I want to see other dimensions of you, Adonai
A dimension of glory and power
Feel these dimensions in my life
Living it with you by my side
May my thoughts be attached to your kingdom
Change me, oh, God
Transform me, my Lord
May your word come to life in my heart
Make me a soldier for your glory
The soldier of eternity.

Lord, come to our rescue
Change us, renew us
All of it to be fit
To receive your thoughts, your priorities
Break our disbelief
Broaden our vision of eternal things
And our desire to live them now
'Cause your Spirit in us is alive and well
Your spirit is a power that lives within us
And is able to do great things
For your glory and your kingdom
We want to see miracles
That you have done with your people
In Egypt when they were captive
Because you haven't changed, Lord
And your kingdom is not just about
In words but in power
You are powerful, oh, my God
And the source of this power
Live in us, it is your Holy Spirit.

I feel oppressed, my God
Filled with doubt and uncertainty
Enlighten me, oh, God
Show me the way
In all this turmoil
Everything is confused in my head
I don't recognize myself anymore
I'm lost, my emotions take over
My faith diminishes, I lose my bearings
I shout to you, Jesus, because only you can help me
My identity is inside you
Enlighten me, my Lord
Because you are not a God of confusion
Drive away all these harmful thoughts
Direct my eyes to you to receive heavenly thoughts
In order to find my peace.

Why so much hatred in my heart
I can't find the way back
My heart is saddened
This burden is so heavy
I am exhausted, Lord
The pain is eating away at me
I'm gradually sinking into the darkness
Oh, Jesus, come to my rescue
Free me from my addiction
This burden that clogs me
And disturbs my sleep
Break my chains
Because only you have the key
God, you're the only one who knows the magic formula
To deliver me and transform me
Teach me to forgive
To make peace with myself and others
I want to live in harmony
Be transformed with your love and free from my ghosts
'Cause only you are my, Jesus, light
An eternal and heavenly light.

Come to my rescue, Jesus
I feel so alone
I'm desperate
My heart is empty
Fill this blank, oh, God
Take your place in my life again
I want to know your joy, oh, God
The peace that comes from heaven
Take me to the source
In order to find meaning in my life, Jesus
I want to receive what you have for my life
Take my hand, draw me to you, Father
Fill me with your mind
Give me this joy of living, Lord
The one that comes from you and lasts forever.

The joy of living comes from you, oh, my God
This inner peace that I feel
I find it only in your presence
When I lie empty, alone
I come to recharge my energy in your presence and in your word
Nothing in this world can satisfy me
Neither silver, nor gold, nor diamonds
This world is ephemeral, Lord
But your world is eternal
I know so little of your world, Jesus
I can't stop asking for more
You are God
You know what I need
Because you are my creator, my God
The master of my life
You wish to fill me with your presence
Of this peace and eternal joy
Thank you, Lord, for your presence.

I want to be happy, Lord
But I can't do it
I seek happiness in the world and in wealth
I'm exhausted from chasing this joy
My eyes are not fixed in the right place, my God
You are the God of joy
Renew my thoughts, restore my confidence
I want to believe in you
To abandon myself completely to you
You alone are my source of joy
I beg your pardon
For my stubbornness and obstinacy
To seek my joy in the world
You're the only one who can fill me and transform me
True happiness is found in you, Jesus.

This suffering and pain that I feel
At the death of a loved one of mine is immense
I feel depressed and sad
To the idea that I couldn't see again
This person who is so precious to me in this world
But at the same time, it reminds me
That I am only passing through on this earth
I can't control my life, Lord
You are the one who holds my destiny in your hands
I am on a mission on this earth
I'm just a visitor to this world
To fulfill my destiny and work for your kingdom
Open my eyes, my God
To see reality and take action to accomplish my mission
I want to answer the call you put on my life
I don't want to waste time on trivia
Because my days on this earth are numbered
But eternal life awaits me with you
Thank you, Jesus, for this promise
Thank you for your Holy Spirit
Who comforts us in these difficult times
And helps us to get up again to continue your work
Hallelujah for eternal life.

The immensity of your greatness
Show me that I am nothing
Come and show me your greatness
Open my eyes to your kingdom
I want to see your power work in my life and around me
May your glory shine on earth
I want to see your miracles, my Lord
I don't want to just be satisfied with your word
But to see your glory and power
Lord, I want to see more
Inexplicable things
That are beyond my comprehension
You want to achieve great things in our lives
But we will have to have faith and desire
To see your power take place in our lives
Open our eyes to the vastness of your kingdom
Touch our hearts to be ready to see your glory
To manifest in and around our lives
In order to recognize that you are a powerful and living God.

Vanity of vanities, all is vanity
Sitting on my bed
Eyes fixed on the sky
I think back on my life
To all that I have received and done
I realize that none of these matters to you
Since all is vanity and pursuit of the wind
Nothing is new under the sky
Everything already existed before I was born
I turn to you, oh, God
So that you can teach me your ways
Direct my eyes to you alone
Put your hand on me
Open my eyes so that I can cling to you
For I am only passing through this earth
One day, I will stand before you, my God
Give me a heart full of joy and gratitude
Since all is vanity
But you are real, my God
May your name be exalted.

Sweet Holy Spirit, come and fill us with your presence
Surround us with your arms of love and kindness
Yes, Lord, you are the true God
The one, the only
The Saint of saints
The King of kings
We place our lives in your hands
Fill us with your peace and your joy of life.
In you, we are more than winners
Oh, God, lay your hand on us
Fill us with your presence
Encourage us in your ways
Guide us by your hand
Accompany us on the road to eternity
Where your presence is omnipresent.

Whoever follows me will be saved
I would give him my water
This water that revitalizes and revives
This water that transforms and renews
He will drink eternally at the source
I am the water of life
Water that will quench your thirst
Water that won't dry up
Water of power and glory
This water is my Holy Spirit
Be filled with my water of life
Because I am at the door.

Oh, my God, I am nothing without you
Come and touch me
Show me the light
I'm so blinded that I can't see anything
I am looking for peace, but I cannot find it in this world
Oh, Jesus, my heart cries out
I feel empty, come and take your place
Free me from the darkness
I can't do it on my own
Oh, Jesus, show me your way
The way to your glory
Thank you for your love
Thank you for your words, my God.

Nations are trembling, the world is afraid
They don't know who to turn to
The world weeps, my God
He doesn't know what to do
But you are here, Jesus
Close to those who are looking for you
You surround your children with your blood
You give us your peace
Eternal peace
So the source is only you, Jesus
Open our eyes, my God
On the immensity of your greatness
Fill us with your heavenly thoughts
Because we have the confidence in you
Since we are not from the world
Blessed be thy name, Jesus, for everlasting life.

Respect to you, Jesus
Glory to your name
I come to your feet
To adore and praise you
Oh, Jesus, you are my savior
My redeemer and my friend
What a beautiful friend I have in my life
A faithful and fair friend
The one who encourages me on difficult days and gets me up
again when I fall
The one who transforms and restores me every day
I want to be at your feet, Jesus
Shouting your name while giving all the respect you deserve
Forgive me, my God
Majesty is your name, high is your person
I am under your shadow, Jesus
Sheltered under your wings and protection
What joy to proclaim your name
I want to stay close to you
Take my hand, Lord, and lead me on your way
The path to eternity
Where your peace resides eternally
Thank you, God, for eternal life.

Reassure me by your presence
Restore me through your love
Sanctify me by your spirit
Remove all worry from my heart and mind
Oh, Jesus, you are my therapist and my psychologist
Without you, toxic thoughts will invade me
Sin will enter my house
My life will have no meaning
But you came knocking at my door
I invited you into my life and you touched me
I will always remember this day
He was exceptional and incredible
My eyes had opened
My vision of the world has changed
Your light has enlightened me
I felt transformed, renewed
The darkness has disappeared, I feel I am alive again
Hallelujah, Adonai
Thank you, Jesus, for this gift
The gift of eternal life.

I am in a total weakness
I can't do anything on my own
To get me out of this mess
Lord, I am lost
Riddled with doubt and anxiety
I can no longer find my way
I refused to follow the light, and now I'm lost
My disobedience is so great that it blinds me
I want to do everything by myself
I try to reason and discuss your decisions for my life
I forget that you are God, my creator
And that I know nothing
Without you, Jesus, I wouldn't be able to get by
Come to my rescue, oh, God
I find myself in the darkness
Because of my disobedience and arrogance
Come and enlighten me, Adonai
I want to leave everything at your feet
Learning to walk in obedience
Because that's what you want from me.

Where two or three meet
I am here among you
Be united for my work
The love you have for me
Must touch what surrounds you
My love for you is infinite
I want you to live in harmony
And that you walk together for my work and my glory
Eliminate any spirit that divides you
Chase away any spirit of lies
I want you to walk hand in hand
I call on all my people to be united for my kingdom
Love one another
Encourage yourself for my work
Be in joy and peace
Walk together, for there is strength in numbers
Alone, you are only a part of my body
But together, you are complete
You represent my whole body
May love be your slogan
Be united and do everything out of love for me
Because I am a God full of love.

Believe in me, have faith
I am here among you
I want to heal you
I want to free you from your burdens
I have carried all your burdens to the cross
You don't need to wear them
Lay at my feet your sufferings and sorrows
I want to set you free
Glorify my name
Invoke my name
I will show you my power
Cause I am the God of the impossible
No one can compare to me
I want to work miracles among you
So that the whole world knows that I am powerful
A living and merciful God
Believe and you will receive your deliverance.

Your word is alive, Lord
It is complex and contains many secrets of your kingdom
It is complete and so beautiful
Oh, my God, enlighten me with your Spirit
To understand this jewel of your kingdom
That you gave us for free
Your word brings me back to life
It restores and renews me
Without your word, I would be lost
She guides me and enlightens me a little more about you
Your kingdom and your thoughts for my life
Thank you, God, for this beautiful gift
Thank you for your heavenly thoughts
That you show me through your word
Glory be to you for your Spirit that enlightens me and brings
light to your writings
Thank you for letting me know your holy scriptures.

You are so great, my God
Wonderful is your name
You calm me in the storm
And fill me with your presence
You quench my thirst with your brandy
I feel rejuvenated in your presence
Fill me with your Spirit
In order to make the works you like
I want to be used, Jesus
For your kingdom and your glory
What an honor to serve you, my God
What a grace to know you
You fill me up, my Lord
I feel alive in your presence
I want to stay at your feet forever.

Blessed be your name, Jesus
My hope is in you
You are the master of my destiny
Without you, I would be lost
You have enlightened and guided me
Cause only you are the way
Without you, I wouldn't know who I am
I would be swallowed up in darkness
You found me and showed me the way to life
Thank you, Jesus, for being there for me
I have done nothing to deserve your grace and kindness
Glory be to our savior
Alleluia, Emmanuel.

I can't imagine spending my life on this earth
Without knowing you, my God
You created me to adore and glorify you
I am your beloved child
Your love for me is so great
That you leave me the choice
To decide what I want
I am free to choose between good and evil
But you show me the way to take, Jesus
In order to have access to eternal life
And this way is you, Jesus
You are the only good in this world
You created me so that I may walk in your ways
And do well around me
Even if I am free to make my own choices
I want to do what you want and not follow the world or the
darkness
Come and enlighten me, Jesus, open my eyes
So that I may choose the path of life
Because by myself, I couldn't get out of it.

I want to honor you with my life, Lord
Because it belongs to you
My existence on this earth depends on you and your goodness
Take my life, Jesus, it belongs to you
I know nothing, but you know everything
You created me for your glory, Adonai
I kneel before you
Come and do the right thing, Jesus
To transform myself in your image
In order to be able to do your work
I want to get up to follow you and answer your call
Walking in my destiny
Fighting the good fight with faith and the sword of the spirit
That you gave me for free
By your grace and love
I want to send your army away, my God
The one who fights for the works of heaven
In order to establish your kingdom and destroy the works of
the evil one
You chose me, Jesus, and I want to be ready
When you come back for us
In all your glory and power.

I raise my voice to worship and praise you
Words fail me to describe your glory and power
Excellent is your name, Lord
I want to lift you up and exalt you
Oh, Jesus, you're wonderful
Your name is so big
It gives me so much joy
I want to jump and shout your name wherever I go
Savior of humanity, creator of heaven and earth
I glorify you and sing your name
Cause you are God
The one, the only
The one who resources and revives me
In your presence, I feel alive and revived
This fire that burnt in me
Comes only from you
I want to cheer you and sing your praises
Thank you for the life, Adonai.

Where I am
There is peace and happiness
I am all
The creator, the sovereign
The saint of saints
The King of kings
Blessed be the one who praises me and seeks me
With faith and with all his heart
I am the one who strengthens
And guides you into an unknown world
A powerful and beautiful kingdom
Where my glory and my light reign
Blessed is he who seeks me
For his response will be great.

You are such a wonderful God
Filled with love and peace
I love your presence, Lord
It fills me up and reassures me
Near you, I feel light
Carefree and stress-free
I feel soothed in your presence
You are the master of peace and the best psychologist, Lord
My therapy is in you, my God
I want to drink at the source
Leaving my burden at the foot of the cross
Admire your works and your presence in my life
Words fail me to describe the good you do me, Lord
I know that this blessing comes from you, Jesus
You carried everything for me
Blessed be your name, Jesus.

Here is the dawn of a new day coming up
A new day, a new adventure
A new prophecy and new revelations
You are a God of surprises
Every day, you show us a new facet
Of your person and your power
How great you are, my God
Majestic is your name
I love all your facets, my God
I want to find out more about them
For I know so little of your magnificence and power
I want to learn more about you
Dispose of my heart to receive your revelations with joy and
faith
These revelations are of great importance because they come
from you
Oh, my God, you are so good
Nothing is new for you
But everything is new to me
'Cause you are my creator
And you mean everything to me
Surprise me, Lord
I want to be amazed every day
By your power and greatness
I want to testify to the whole world that you are God
The one and only
The living God and in your son there is life
Glory be to you, my God.

I love to hear you, my God
The voice of eternity
When you talk to me, it touches me and transforms me
What happiness to hear your voice, Lord
It is wonderful, soft, strengthening, and comforting
When you talk to me, I live again
All my is in a deep and indescribable joy
My soul recognizes the voice of his creator and submits itself
I love to listen to you, my God
This melodious voice that fills me with peace
This is the voice of my savior
You take the time to visit me and talk to me
I am all ears, my God
Ready to receive your revelations and prophecies
I want to take your orders and stand up to carry them out
I like it when you give me missions for your kingdom
I feel alive when you talk to me
Thank you, God, for taking the time to talk to me
Forgive my disobedience
Entrust me with the tasks for your kingdom
Cause I was born for it
I am a soldier of eternity not of the world
You are my God and my creator
My soul sighs after you
Come and fill him up, my God.

Christmas Party Bonus

What's Christmas?
It's not a Christmas tree party or a garland party
Our savior was born in a stable
He was not born in a forest surrounded by fir trees and snow
Or in a sophisticated hospital
He was born in a place full of animals
We tend to think of Christmas as a gift celebration
We even go into debt to offer gifts to everyone
Yet Jesus did not live crowned with extravagant gifts
The film industry sees Christmas as a season of encounters
We meet Prince Charming
We fall in love and get married
But in reality, no one likes to get married in the middle of winter and at negative 20 degrees Celsius
The birth of Jesus is not a time of marriage or encounter.
On the contrary, if we see Jesus's journey, we feel a little sadness
Born in a stable, exiled
Crucified on a cross
You can see that this is not romance
But behind these sufferings lie great works of art
He is our savior, our redeemer, a faithful friend, a guide
And especially our door to heaven
The question we must ask ourselves when celebrating Christmas
Is to know if we really know Jesus
If not, it is not too late
Because he wants to know us
So let's trust him with our lives and tell him today
Yes, I want to follow you, Jesus.

About the Author

Hara Saadia lives in Moncton (Canada). She has been saved since childhood, and she is passionate about the presence of God. She loves to teach the word of God that is why she is a teacher and director of children's ministry in her local church. She is also passionate about gospel music. She has written songs, and some are in production. Her slogan is, "Believe to live the biblical scriptures." It is a phrase that she repeats to herself daily because, yes, she wants to believe in our God and His Son, Jesus, more in order to live what He has in store for her.

The texts that are part of this book were received during her times of personal prayer, worship, and meditation and with others. They are words of encouragement and meditation. Some texts speak of the greatness of God, others of His peace in difficult times, and the importance of obedience in our Christian walk.